Better LETTER WRITING

by Christopher Jarman

Published by Osmiroid International Ltd.

**Published by Osmiroid
International Ltd.,Gosport,
Hampshire, England.**

ISBN 0 9502222 4 0

© **Osmiroid International Ltd., 1989**

No part of this publication may be reproduced, transmitted, recorded or stored in a retrieval system in any form whatsoever without the written permission of the publishers.

Contents

	Page
Introduction	5
Layout of Letters	6
Rough Notes and Copies	9
Handwriting	10
Methods of Address	13
Addressing Envelopes	15

PERSONAL LETTERS

Personal Letters	18
Invitations	20
Thank you Letters	23
Congratulations	25
Sympathy and Condolence	27
Complaints	30
Love Letters	34

BUSINESS LETTERS

Business Letters	38
Internal Memos	42
Job Applications	45
Testimonials and References	51
Letters to the Press	54
Writing to your M.P.	57
Conclusion	58
Range of Nibs	59

Introduction

Letters are important to us all for many different reasons, a personal letter can become a keepsake, a reminder that a friend or loved one cares enough to put their thoughts on paper, personal letters should be interesting, informative and wherever possible, fun to read. Business letters must be brief, to the point and correct to be effective. "Better LETTER WRITING" recognises that personal and business correspondence require different approaches and so you will find this book clearly divided into two sections.

A good letter can get you a job interview, it can sell your product, it can give you the time to think how to best present a difficult message. "Better LETTER WRITING" aims to show you how.

Layout of Letters

There are three common types of layout normally used today. When writing a letter by hand it does not matter which you decide to use. In fact handwritten letters may be written in circles or spirals or any other artistic forms that you believe the recipient may enjoy! On the whole, however, unless you know the person you're writing to very well, it is best to use a fairly standard layout.

1. Modern business letter layout for busy typists, with straight left-hand margins.

K-Colora

Unit 6
St Andrews Industrial Estate
Winton
Hampshire W86 3JD

Telephone 55190
Telex 477843

Directors: C Jones   N Long   J Hepenstal

B R Blue Esq
Colormix PLC
Green Lane
Redcliffe B1 2CR

Our Ref CJ/MH/3

Date 04.06.87

Dear Barry

Thank you for your letter of 2nd. I was delighted to hear that you had landed the contract in Auckland.

We will be sending you samples of our own colorboxes and colorpens in about three weeks and I should be grateful to know what you think of them.

Do not worry about the lack of full stops and commas in the address. This is the modern business way for speed.

All good wishes

Yours sincerely

Colin Jones

2. The traditional layout more suited to personal correspondence with indented paragraphs.

```
                              Mrs K Miller
                              Flat 6A
                              Park Mews
                              Godalming
                              Surrey     GUX 14

                           Tel: 04860

                              Thursday 8th September 19 -
```

Dear Ralph,

    I so enjoyed meeting you the other evening at Sarah's party, and an otherwise boring evening went by in a flash.

    You quite forgot to ask my address and so you will see I am sending it to you.

    We are having some friends in for a few drinks next Sunday at 11 o'clock before lunch. I do hope you can come. Please write or ring to say yes.

        Yours in anticipation

Kathleen

Kathleen

3. Informal handwritten layout with extended paragraphs suitable for flourished capitals if desired.

          Flat 6A, Park Mews, Godalming, Surrey GU14.
                    Telephone 04860
                        Sunday

My dearest Ralph,

    I shall never forget the wonderful Sunday lunch & afternoon. The flowers you brought are still in front of me smelling absolutely heavenly.
    You are such a thoughtful person to have made such an impression on my mother. She said she likes you which is unheard of until now!
    Please let me know when we can see each other again. I simply adore Italian food.

                Yours very affectionately,
                      Katie

Rough Notes and Copies

It is always a good idea when planning a difficult letter, whether for business or personal reasons, to make a rough list of what you intend to say. Simply put on a sheet of paper in any order, the vital points.

For example, say you are writing to ask for an improvement grant. You might jot down the following:

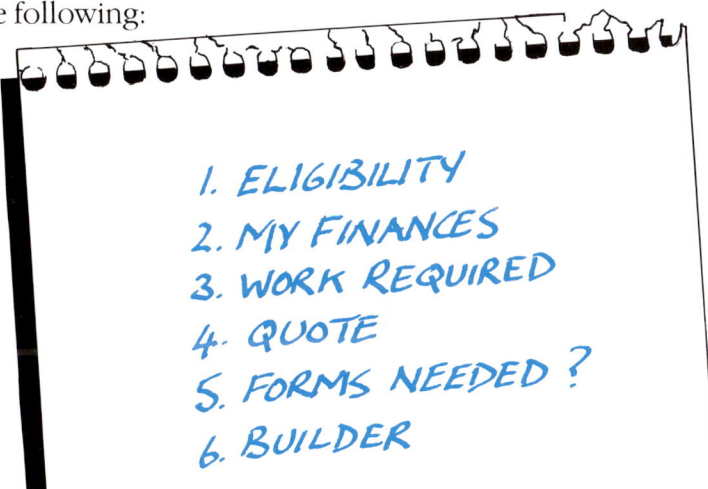

1. ELIGIBILITY
2. MY FINANCES
3. WORK REQUIRED
4. QUOTE
5. FORMS NEEDED?
6. BUILDER

When you write the letter you may decide to rearrange the list and mention the six points in a better order, perhaps starting off with the work required. This brief exercise will help to clarify your thinking for any type of letter which is not absolutely simple to write. Also, if you want to take a day or two to think the letter over, the list helps you to remember the points you wished to make when you finally get down to writing it.

Copies

In these days of cheap and efficient photocopying it is easy for those who work in offices to make copies of letters before mailing them. However, there are some drawbacks. Some heavily tinted notepapers and some coloured inks (especially blue) do not photocopy easily. For photocopying, black ink on white paper is always best. For people at home without access to copying machines, remember the traditional carbon paper is still good both for handwritten and typed copies. There are also pads of self-copying paper which are very useful for ballpoint written letters. Remember to place a sheet of card under the last copy sheet each time!

With modern electronic typewriters and home word processors, the chip memory can be used to produce as many top quality copies as you need.

Handwriting

Good readable handwriting is not only good manners, it is good business. Many business people judge job applicants and requests for interviews and so on, by the quality of the handwriting. Most people are more impressed by legibility than by flowing flourishes and decorations in handwriting.

Our modern handwriting is based upon a joined form of Roman lower case alphabet which was developed over 1000 years ago. The most basic and historically accurate shape of handwriting consists of letters made up of slightly sloping ovals and parallel lines.

I O I O I O I O I

There are only eight patterns to be practised in order to train the hand and eye to write clearly. These can be used to improve your writing whatever style you may have used until now. They are shown with the letters that each pattern is designed to help and improve.

mmmmmmm	r n m h b p k
c ccccccccc	c o a g d q e
uuuuuuuu	i u y t
/\/\/\/\/\/\/\/\	v w x
ululululul	i u l y t d
mmmmmm	r n m p

ooooooo *oo oa od og*

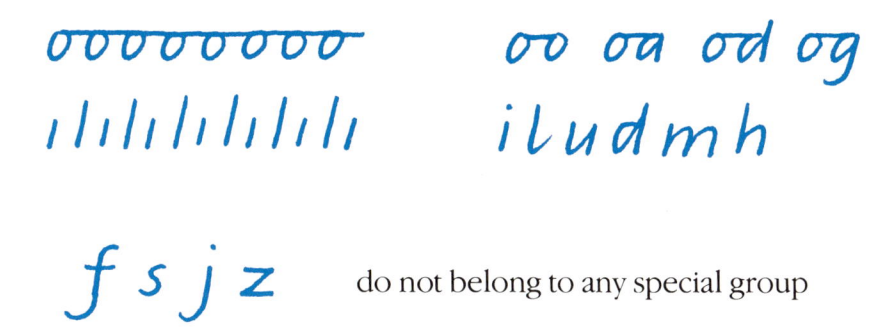

ı lı lı lı lı lı lı *i l u d m h*

f s j z do not belong to any special group

Joining Letters

Good handwriting is always cursive, that is "running" or joined up. The printing of letters separately should never be taught in schools. Indeed before 1913 writing for even the youngest children was always taught joined up from the beginning.

There are two kinds of join,
1. **Horizontal**

wood top two on vote from fox of vow food

2. **Diagonal**

main came do his and mum animal

The following letters are best left unjoined, as the pen ends up at the end of each letter in an inconvenient position for joining.

b g j p q y s

Capital Letters

These should always be based upon the plain Roman capitals and should be no taller than the ascenders of l h d b and k. Capitals need not be joined to small letters unless the join occurs naturally. Capitals are never joined to one another.

Some practice with capitals and joins:

Anne Bill Cathy Don Edgar Freddy Gale Helen Isaac Joe Kevin Lorna Mike Nan Oscar Pauline Quentin Rod Sue Tom Ursula Val Will Xerxes Zeb

Methods of Address

Both the look of the name and address on the envelope and the start of a letter are very important. These give the first impression of you, or the organisation you represent. Little things like a mistaken initial, omitting a hyphen, or getting a qualification wrong can cause quite unreasonable offence at times.

The safest and most courteous form of address in a letter today is either "Dear Sir" or "Dear Madam". This applies to those with all kinds of other titles, peers, clergy, etc. Always try to find out in advance whether your addressee is male or female as Dear Sir/Madam is acceptable but rather impersonal. Such an opening should be matched by the formal closure "Yours faithfully". If you write Dear Mr. Brown, or Dear Mary, (using a name,) then the closure will be "Yours sincerely".

The way to begin a letter to the following recipients – whether male or female is:

> **Dear Dr Grant,**
> **Dear Professor Hunt,**
> **Dear Canon Perkins,**
> **Dear Lord Brent,**
> **Dear Lieutenant Pratt,**
> **Dear Admiral Smith,**

for Knights or Dames use the first name always:

> **Dear Dame Louise,**
> **Dear Sir Keith,**
> **Dear Lady Sarah,**

All these will close with **"Yours sincerely".**

If someone is known as the "Honourable" they should be addressed as Dear Sir, Dear Madam or Dear Mr. or Mrs. and then their surname. Of course, if you know the recipient well, you may prefer to use Yours truly, Yours ever, As ever, etc.

When putting letters after a person's name the rule is that the following awards come after the name in this order of procedure. First the Victoria Cross, VC, GC, (George Cross), KG, (Knight of the Garter), PC, (Privy Counsellor), the KCB, KCVO, CB. Service medals are put in the following order DSC, MC, DFC, AFC, DCM, CGM, DSM, MM, DFM, BEM.

If anyone is a Member of Parliament 'MP' this always comes last. Justice of the Peace 'JP', is put just before 'MP' if the addressee is both. University degrees are not usually added in ordinary correspondence. However, if the recipient is in a profession where degrees are particularly relevant such as teaching, medicine, or the law, it may be prudent to put degrees on the envelope at least. These are added in order of status, the *lowest* first i.e. BA, MA, M.Phil, Ph.D, and should come after decorations and orders.

Note that no full stops are put between abbreviations of titles, just commas to separate each different title.

Addressing Envelopes

The first impression of your letter is the envelope. While an economy label reusing an old envelope with the message 'Save a tree' may be fine for a letter to your best friend, it will not advance your reputation if sent for a job application!

Addresses should always be written with the envelope horizontal and if it has a side flap, leave this to the left.

Always start the address half-way down the envelope to leave plenty of space for stamps and franking or airmail stickers. If you wish to write PERSONAL or CONFIDENTIAL on the envelope, do this to the left above the name.

When writing to someone at a large organisation which may be on several sites such as an industrial complex or university, make sure you put the department or office as there may be hundreds of internal alternative destinations. Always put the post-code if there is one, as the last line on the address.

A well addressed envelope may look like this:

```
PERSONAL


                    Fred Thimble Esq., FCA
                     Accounts Office
                      Wellside Furniture Stores
                       BOOTHAVEN
                         Dorset        BH14 2QR
```

On a large envelope or package it is a good idea to put the senders name and address on the envelope too. The American convention is to put this on the top left-hand corner of the envelope. The British way is to write it on the back of the envelope prefixed clearly by the word "From". "Mr." is a more common form of address than "Esq." nowadays.

Personal Letters

Personal Letters

These days personal letters are very informal. The telephone call has replaced many such communications, but sometimes a friend or a loved one is too far away to call. The main thing is to relax and be natural. Just say what you really want to say in the simplest words. Put yourself in the other person's place and think what he or she would most like to read. Some useful tips if you are stuck are:

1. Describe what you have been doing at work, at school, at the weekend.
2. Write about a book, news, or TV programme you have enjoyed.
3. Give news about mutual friends, or relatives, old school friends. What happened to so and so?
4. Tell the latest joke you have heard.
5. Ask questions about their job, family and events.
6. If you feel strongly about some things don't hesitate to say so, but if you are criticising remember to read it over again before sending it.
7. Don't forget little sketches and drawings, pieces of verse and decoration. These all help to make a personal letter more entertaining.

A letter from one person direct to another should be straightforward and direct. Think out exactly what it is you want to say and write it. Such old-fashioned phrases as "I trust you are well" or "hoping this reaches you in good health" are today an indication of a lack of experience both in writing and in the use of English. A good way to start is to thank the person for writing to you or for sending a gift or card if they have. This reassures them that you have had their communication and that they have sent it to the right address. These days people move about much more than they used to and getting new addresses correct is important. For this reason it is not only good manners but very important to put your own address clearly at the top of personal letters. Always put the date on your letters. Many years later it could be extremely valuable to be able to date even the most light-hearted letter if it has been kept.

Try not to apologise too much in personal letters, or to emphasise how busy or overworked you are. It does not as a rule elicit sympathy. It merely seems as if you are begrudging the time taken to write.

If you have any strong criticisms to make, it is very helpful to write them down in a rough form and wait a day or so.

Then read what you have said over again and generally re-phrase it more diplomatically when the heat of the moment has gone. Never write an abusive or libellous letter. It will not serve any good purpose and is likely to do the writer more harm than the recipient.

Invitations

More formal personal letters, such as invitations, congratulations, condolences, etc. need a little more thought. They need not be long. Just long enough to serve their purpose is usual.

The standard formal invitation is usually printed on a card and states:

> Mr and Mrs Dennis Bailey
> Request the pleasure of
>
> ....
>
> company
> at Dinner on
> Wednesday, 4th August at 8.00pm
>
> 12 Fairmont Row,
> Woodstock.
> RSVP

Otherwise, invitations today are mostly quite informal, notes beginning Dear Susan or Dear Mr. and Mrs. Skinner, etc. Some useful phrases for invitations are:

1. It would be so nice if you could join us ....
2. We would be so pleased if you could come to ....

3. John/Mary and I would so love to see you for supper/dinner etc.........

4. Will you give us the pleasure of your company on ....

5. We are having a few friends over on Friday and should be delighted if you could come too ....

6. We are hoping to have a party/dance/picnic and we want you to come as it would not be comlete without you.

Example of Invitations and reply to a formal party
(engagement, 18th birthday, (wedding anniversary, etc.)

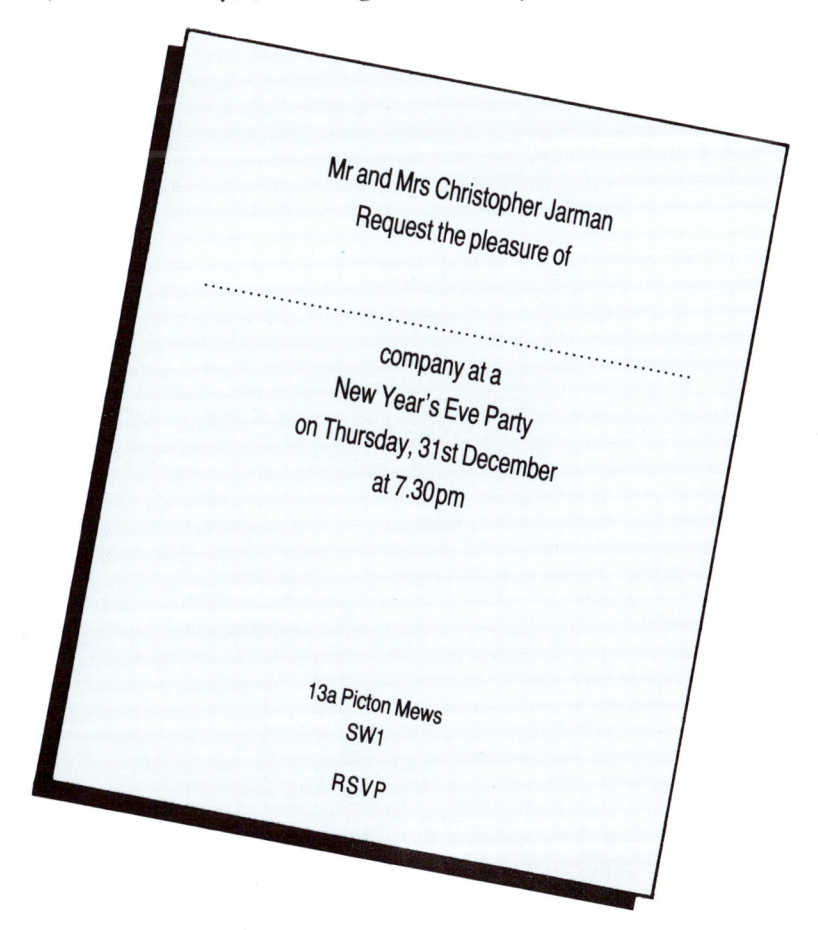

> Mr and Mrs Christopher Jarman
> Request the pleasure of
>
> ....
>
> company at a
> New Year's Eve Party
> on Thursday, 31st December
> at 7.30pm
>
> 13a Picton Mews
> SW1
>
> RSVP

The formal reply to this type of invitation is:

> 12 Beverley Road,
> London,
> SW15
>
> Miss Agatha Brown thanks Mr and Mrs Christopher Jarman for their kind invitation to their New Year's Eve Party and has much pleasure in accepting.

OR

> 12 Beverley Road,
> London,
> SW15
>
> Miss Agatha Brown thanks Mr and Mrs Christopher Jarman for their kind invitation to their New Year's Eve Party and much regrets she is unable to attend as she has another engagement.

Thank you Letters

Thank you letters are probably amongst the most important letters we write. Yet they are the ones most frequently avoided or allowed to lapse until it is too late. Many older relatives, godparents and friends are genuinely hurt and anxious when no letter of thanks arrives after a gift or a visit. In particular when money or valuables have been sent by post a thank you letter is vital as a check that they have been received.

Presents are exciting to receive, but they are likely to be gradually discontinued when the courtesy of a thank you letter is not returned.

If you have difficulty in wording a thank you, here is a short checklist of starting phrases:

I am extremely grateful for ....

Many thanks for ....

I greatly appreciate your generosity ....

I really must thank you for ....

It was so kind of you to ....

I am writing at once to thank you ....

Please accept my sincere thanks for ....

It was very good of you to ....

Always write thank yous by hand and either use an attractive decorated notelet or your best headed notepaper. It is not necessary for it to be a long letter. If it was a dinner party given by a couple you should write to the hostess.

Even the youngest children can be encouraged to write brief thank you letters. It is not only good social training it is very much in their own interests. A child's letter can be very short.

> *Navy D80*
>
> Dear Uncle Nigel
> Thankyou for the present.
> love from
> Stuart

Perhaps with a drawing as well. Incidentally it is always more helpful for a child to draw first and then write about the drawing. This helps to make the idea more clear in a child's mind. It is much more successful than saying "When you have written the letter you can do a drawing."

Congratulations

Letters of this sort are both a pleasure to write and to receive. It is always best to keep the letter to the topic in hand, and not dilute the joy by discussing your backache or the political situation.

Before leaping in to congratulate a friend on getting engaged, married or pregnant, it is worthwhile checking up that all parties are actually happy about it. The same with the birth of a child. The seventeen-year-old unmarried mother or a fifty-year-old father landed with an 'afterthought' may not always appreciate a fulsome letter of ecstacy.

Never refer to previous attachments, liaisons or marriages in your letter of congratulations. Let the new life begin without looking back. It is so easy to be unintentionally hurtful by even slight references. As in all correspondence always remember that more than one person will usually read your letter. What may be a harmful comment well understood by your friend may not be appreciated by their partner or relatives.

If writing to a younger person or child to congratulate them on passing an exam, or getting a job, avoid making it the excuse for a lecture on hard work and diligence. This will inevitably spoil the impact of the letter. Much better to enclose a small cheque to say 'Go out and celebrate'.

Here is a checklist of phrases to help start a letter of congratulations.

> We were so pleased to hear ....
>
> Do accept my/our congratulations on ....
>
> May I as an old friend send you my congratulations on ....
>
> I have just heard that .... and I wish you every happiness
>
> I am so glad to hear that ....
>
> Congratulations on ....!

A typical letter of congratulations might be:

6 Stillman Place,
Longham,
Surrey.

July 3rd 19-

Dear Mrs White,

   I was delighted to see from the newspaper that you have a son/daughter. You must both feel very proud. I hope you are all making good progress. I look forward to coming to see you as soon as it is convenient.

   Please accept our heartiest congratulations and every good wish.

   Yours very sincerely,

Paul

Paul Jones

Sympathy and Condolence

These are very difficult letters to write and many of us avoid them by convincing ourselves that the person concerned would not want us to intrude. Unless he or she has specifically said so this is very unlikely. In distress or grief it is human nature to want to know that other people care and are sympathetic. However, a person in this state does not want to discuss details and still less to hear how *you* felt when you had *your* tragedy.

What is required in the first instance is the knowledge that you care and sympathise.

One way out is to send one of the many pre-printed sympathy cards which can be bought. For a not too serious illness this can be acceptable. To someone who is bereaved however a short personal note written by hand is much more effective. In particular a brief letter from even a slight acquaintance can be very comforting.

Always put your address and date on all such letters, and put your surname somewhere as in times of stress a letter from 'Alan' or 'Sue' can be totally mystifying however well you think the recipient knows you. He or she may know three or four Alans and Sues.

One example might be:

3 West Way,
Brandon,
Yorkshire.
YD4 6SL

8th February 19-

Dear Mrs Black,

I was sorry to hear of David's death last week. Please accept my deepest sympathy and condolences. I am sure you know how well liked and respected he was in the Society. He will be greatly missed.

Please do not hesitate to ask me if there is anything I can do.

With kindest regards,

Stanley Green.

Stanley Green

No other subjects should be mentioned in a first letter of condolence however important it may seem to you. Leave everything for a week or two and then broach any other vital area of concern.

It is not a good idea to use 'delicate' phrases such as 'passed away' or 'happy release'. It is more comfortable and honest to use normal everyday phrases and words.

Here is a checklist of useful phrases for condolence and sympathy letters:

>   I was shocked to hear of the death of ....
>
>   I have just learned of the death of ....
>
>   I was deeply sorry to hear the news of ....
>
>   Please accept my sympathy during your wife's illness ....
>
>   I was very sorry to hear that your husband has had to go into hospital ....

Letters of this kind may be ended with:
>   Sincere regards
>
>   With kindest regards
>
>   Yours very sincerely
>
>   All our love
>
>   With love
>
>   Love

Whichever you choose depends, of course, on how well you know the recipient.

Complaints

It is easy to sit down and dash off a letter of complaint. It gets the feelings off your chest and often relieves the frustration. Whenever you write a letter like that, never send it. Throw it away and start again. Letters of complaint are meant to achieve your aim, not to let off steam.

The first rule is to put yourself in the other person's place and imagine what sort of a letter would have the right effect. Look at this suggested table of cause – effect

Angry letter –	resentment and anger in return – negative
Threatening letter –	defence, anger, fear, retaliation – negative
Abusive letter –	amusement, pity, disdain – negative
Hurt, whining letter –	scorn, distaste, wastepaper basket – negative
Long earnest list of complaints in detail –	boredom, inaction – negative
Short letter, firm, friendly –	interest – positive
Short letter with calm statement of the facts and specific request for reasonable action, showing understanding of the other person's problem	likely agreement, and positive action

Such phrases as 'I am disgusted', 'disgraceful service' 'appalling conditions' or any other exaggerated language will seldom help a written complaint. They just serve to make even a justifiable anger look silly on paper. An understated conciliatory tone in a letter works wonders. The mere fact that you are writing is usually enough indication of your feelings.

A letter of complaint may be a simple consumer dispute, a complaint to a neighbour or local authority or it may be a serious matter which may precede a full legal complaint or threat of litigation. It is always a good idea to be both polite and brief and merely to state the facts in initial correspondence.

1. **A simple complaint.**

> Dear Sirs,
>
> The chair I ordered from you was delivered today and on unpacking it I discovered a bad stain on the left arm. I cannot possibly accept it in this state and I would be obliged if you would replace it. I shall be at home each morning next week.
>
> Yours faithfully,

2. A complaint which may lead to litigation.

Dear Sirs,
<u>Without Prejudice</u>

I recently contracted with your salvage department to recover my 30 ft. yacht "Destiny" from the beach at Eastbourne.

I have since received a bill for £98-00 plus VAT for "inspecting" the yacht and deciding its salvage was too difficult.

I cannot accept that £98-00 is a fair charge for <u>not</u> salvaging a boat.

I am prepared to offer half that sum as a gesture of goodwill.

I hope that this matter may be settled without further outside advice.

Yours faithfully.

Who to write to

If you are complaining to a neighbour or your local school etc. then write by name to the person concerned. If however, you are complaining to a large organisation such as a Gas Board or Local Authority then you should either find out if there is a specific department for complaint, or address your letter to the Managing Director or Chief Executive. Letters to large organisations are almost invariably opened by a Secretary and often copied or sent round to several departments. Therefore always keep any personal references out of such letters, especially if you know anyone in the organisation, as a letter which is too personal may inhibit its circulation and thus its effectiveness.

Here is a checklist of useful phrases for letters of complaint:

May I call your attention ....

I beg to remind you ....

I regret to have to tell you ....

I am writing to ask if you will agree ....

I am sorry to have to tell you ....

I am extremely disappointed to write in this way but ....

I write to complain about ....

I am really sorry to have to write in this way but ....

In all cases of serious complaints concerning goods or services, you would be well advised to consult yor local Consumer Advice Centre. There are about 200 of these across the country.

Love Letters

These are so personal and private that no rules can apply as to style, address and so on. Collections of the love letters of famous people show us that they may be as innocent, naïve and playful as the rest of us. The main thing is to be yourself and be honest.

Nevertheless, love letters written without any thought of the consequences have caused tremendous difficulties. Like most other letters, it cannot be guaranteed that no one else will read them. Do not let your natural emotions cast out your reason entirely. So there are four rules which are worth bearing in mind even for love letters:

1. Do not make promises which you cannot fulfil or do not intend to fulfil.
2. Remember no letters are guaranteed to be private.
3. Never slander another person.
4. There are laws governing what written/pictorial material may be sent through the mail, and in some countries this is very strict indeed.

It is as well not to put love messages on the outside of the envelope or tired old acronyms such as S.W.A.L.K. These may well embarrass the person receiving the letter and spoil the enchantment. People do not always want their family or the postman to know they are receiving a love letter.

If you cannot think of anything to say, then your loved one may appreciate a poem copied out which expresses your feelings more exactly. Meanwhile as your relationship develops, you will have mutual memories to share and you can begin saying 'Remember when we . . . .'

Examples

From a man:

> Darling,
>
> It is already two hours since we said goodbye and it seems like two weeks. The only thing that will keep me from being utterly miserable until Thursday is your beautiful photograph. I have it in front of me now. I keep it in my desk drawer as I don't want to share you with anyone else.
>
> I tried hard to tell you how much I love you today, but I can never seem to find the right words. I hope that I at least *show* you even though I am rather tongue-tied when I try to speak!
>
> The boss is giving me some funny looks so I must finish this quickly. Can't wait to see you.
>
> Yours very loving
> Garry.

A reply to the previous letter:

Darling Garry,

I am always the first into the post-room to collect the mail these days. Little do they guess why I am so keen. I have a store of your letters locked away and they are quite crumpled from re-reading.

You aren't the only one who is tongue tied. I am much worse; but letters are great aren't they because you can sort your ideas out and organise them. Anyway I think what you say is lovely and I feel I understand you completely when we are together. I don't feel a bit shy when I am with you, just lost for words. It's not the same! I can't wait for Thursday either.

I LOVE YOU

Joan

Business Letters

Business Letters

Writing to your Bank/Building Society/Solicitor/Headteacher/Accountant, etc. When writing to a professional person whom you do not know personally, it is good manners to find out their correct address and status. If they have a degree or professional qualification represented by a group of letters after their name, this should be put on the envelope, and also at the top left-hand side of the letter with the address. The letter should then begin Dear Mr. Brown or Dear Mrs. Smith as appropriate. It is a very useful practice then to put a heading indicating the main content of your letter. Sign this letter Yours sincerely. If your own signature is difficult to read, either type or print your name under it. Always indicate your own sex or status as Mr., Mrs., Miss or Ms. There is nothing more calculating to annoy recipients of letters in business than a signature I. M. Jones with no indication whether it is a man or woman.

Always try to be as brief as possible and use paragraph numbering to make your separate points or questions clear.

Example A

27th October 19-

A. P. Henry, LLB, MA,
Messrs. Henry, Bagg & Lilt, Solicitors,
6/7 High Street,
Woolston,
Lancashire. FG1 6TY

Dear Mr. Henry,

<u>PURCHASE OF 8 FAIRMOUNT TERRACE, WOOLSTON</u>

I enclose a copy of the survey carried out by my Building Society surveyor and I hope this will answer all your questions.

I have three other queries for you, however, they are:

1. Will my unmarried status affect my repayments?
2. Is the leasehold able to be changed to freehold?
3. What are your charges?

I would be grateful for your answers as soon as possible.

                      Yours sincerely,

                      Ann Holden

                      Ann Holden (Miss)

Enclosure.

These days it is important not to use those old fashioned commercial phrases such as 'We beg to acknowledge . . .', 'assuring you of our best attention', 'enclosed herewith', 'will oblige . . .', etc. Use straightforward English as you would face to face. Expressions such as 'ult' for month, and 'inst' for date were abandoned in good business 20 years ago. They merely make your letters seem not only old fashioned, but uneducated as well.

Business letters usually have one or more of these objectives:

1. To achieve some action or results

2. To give information or facts

3. To keep a relationship co-operative

Always try to use short words and short sentences. A little humour or wit is a good thing occasionally. We all like to receive a letter which assumes we are human. Courtesy is vital in a business letter. Rudeness will get you nowhere and may well rebound upon you. However, if someone writes you a dishonest or cheeky letter it does no harm to give a polite but blunt reply. If someone is really trying to put one over you or your organisation, gentle sarcasm is probably your best course. For example if you are being quoted an excessive price for a service or product, you could reply in this vein:

Example B

NIGEL LONG
design

ST. ANDREWS,
PETERSFIELD ROAD,
WINCHESTER,
HAMPSHIRE SO23 8JD.
TELEPHONE (0962) 55190

Mr S Black
Trexton Parts plc
Industrial Estate
Waring
Oxon   OX4 21A

20th June 1988

Your ref MB/BH/881

Dear Mr Black

ESTIMATE FOR REPAIR No. 7240

Thankyou for your quote of 16th June. This is very much higher than we had expected, particularly as we had considered the job to be reasonably straightforward.

If you are really paying your work force the kind of hourly rate your labour costs imply, they must all be coming to work in new BMW's!

We would be grateful if you would kindly review your costs and advise if any savings can be made.

Yours sincerely

Your letterhead, logo, quality of writing paper and general appearance of the typing all convey important signals to the recipient. If you do not think about all these things you do not deserve to be in business. Appearances in this area count very much indeed.

Internal Memos

Memos within an organisation can be boring, ineffective, laughable, counter-productive or political dynamite. They can enhance your position and credibility within the company or they can rebound upon you and cause great distress. Internal memos are probably some of the most important documents you will ever write.

To begin with memos are seldom private and confidential, even though they may be marked so. They are read by secretaries, put into files and are available for months or years afterwards if not destroyed. A good internal memo can help with an executive career, a bad one could cause trouble.

If a memo is written to a senior person criticising a colleague or a procedure designed by a colleague, you are likely to make an enemy or at least to cause offence. If the comment is justified it makes no difference to the result. It would be much better to mention the complaint to the colleague verbally.

A mild reproof or even a pointed question in an internal note with copies to several other people can be a most effective way of embarrassing a person. But do not expect to be popular for it! In the same manner a memo congratulating someone on an achievement or a good idea, goes down very well, and your reputation for generosity will be enhanced. Never send public memos congratulating a senior colleague, however, you will be classed as a crawler. Confine your praise largely to juniors or equals.

Internal memos should always be short. Long notes are classed as 'papers' or 'reports' rather than memos. The most economical business practice is to write 'agree' or 'disagree' or whatever is appropriate at the bottom of a letter or existing memo and return it to the sender. Remember however to take a photocopy if you need a record.

Try to write the kind of memo you would like to receive yourself and that would be effective in making *you* act.

For example

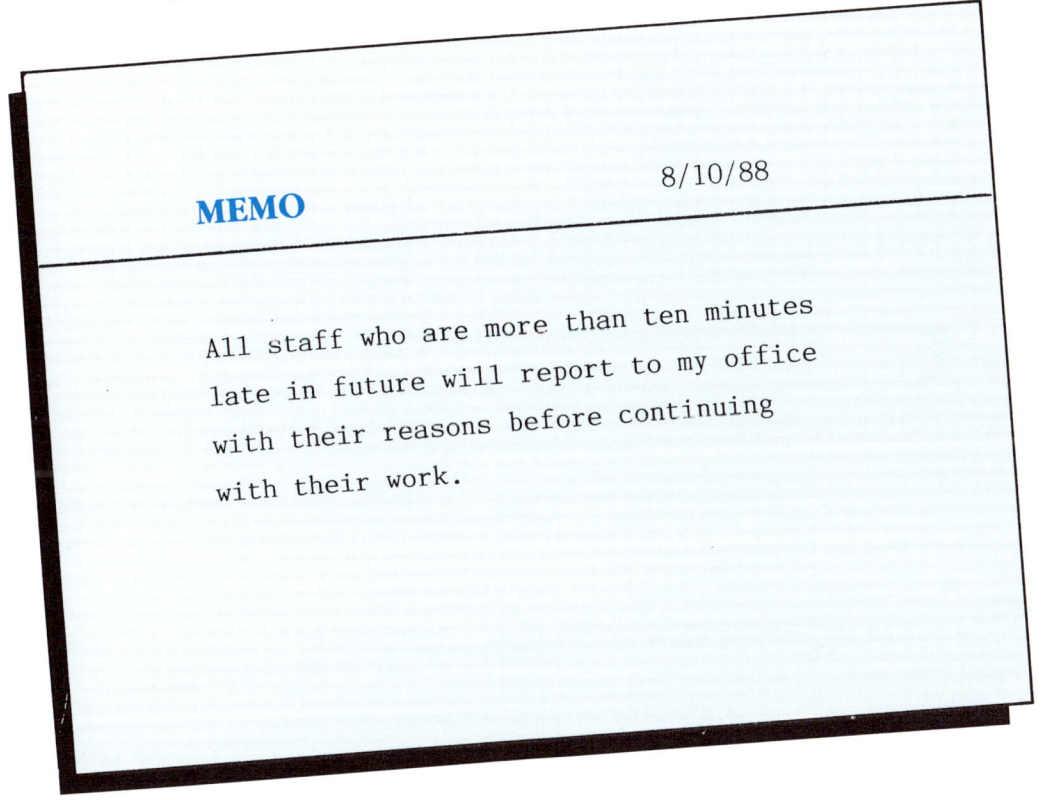

> **MEMO**   8/10/88
>
> All staff who are more than ten minutes late in future will report to my office with their reasons before continuing with their work.

This type of memo is not only too general to be effective, it will cause even more waste of both your time and your employees'. It will frighten the meek and alienate the strong minded, thus lowering morale and efficiency rather than strengthening it. A better memo might be . . .

MEMO 8/10/88

More than two hundred working hours were lost through staff arriving late for work last year. Remember, punctuality actually saves money, and will count towards your promotion in this company.

    This approach gives genuine information and is encouraging, showing leadership. The first memo shows weakness and lack of imagination in retreating behind petty authority.

Job Applications

It has been my good fortune to read hundreds of job applications over the last 20 years and what entertaining reading they make! It is fair to say that at least half the applications received whether on a special form or merely a letter, seem designed to lose the chance of the job.

In general, you must read the advertisement carefully and know exactly what the job is for which you are applying. If it says 'knowledge of French required' do not put 'I speak German'. If shorthand typing is specified then it is fruitless putting yourself forward as a skilled audio typist. Of course you may be lucky, but to the person sorting through dozens of applications it is merely irritating to read.

Unless an advert specifies a handwritten application, always type it or have it typed. If your are proud of your handwriting you can always add a brief handwritten note to show off. Never apply for jobs in green ink or any exotic colours, never apply on coloured or scented notepaper as this is most unbusinesslike and hardly conducive to shortlisting. Remember also that it is hard to photocopy coloured inks and paper and almost all applications are copied and circulated these days. Thus even blue ink is unwise as it photocopies badly.

If the organisation sends you their own application form, use it. It means they have a system which it fits and that they particularly want the answers to those questions. If a question is not applicable or you do not wish to answer it, just write N/A (not applicable) in the space provided. *It is always a good idea to add a brief accompanying letter.* No prospective employer objects to this. It shows keenness and intelligence, and can add information which is not on the form. Nevertheless the letter must be typed and not more than one side of A4 paper if possible. Do *not* write a chatty handwritten note on small sized notepaper, these slip down between standard A4 sheets, are hard to read and can cause annoyance to the busy selectors.

A good accompanying letter will be businesslike, crisp, use short paragraphs, and may contain some easily expressed statistics. Here are two examples of the style which would be very likely to gain you an interview.

Example A

34 East Road,
Weston,
Hampshire.

25 June 198-

The Secretary,
Bunhaven Leisure Parks,
Hampton,
Surrey.

Dear Secretary,

<u>ASSISTANT MANAGER - APPLICATION</u>

I enclose my completed application form for your consideration. In addition I would like to add the following information.

1. During my eight years in the Royal Navy I served in five warships and was appointed entertainments officer in each one. I have arranged functions for embassy staff and local notables in the following cities; Mombasa, Sydney, Wellington and Naples.

2. I have arranged the following courses and conferences during my present job as educational assistant to Somerset County Council:

   35 Weekend Conferences for teachers
   26 Summer Schools for social workers
   10 Evening Courses for clergy

I would be happy to bring brochures confirming these points and other documentation to an interview.

Yours faithfully,

Edward Brown.

Edward Brown

Enclosure.

14 Valley Road
Boston
Norfolk

The Managing Director
Frozen Foods plc
Haversham
Norfolk

25th June 198-

Dear Sir

<u>COMPANY SECRETARY - APPLICATION</u>

I enclose my completed application form for your consideration. In addition I would like to add the following information.

1. Although I have been working abroad for the past four years, it was with a lively Swiss company which sent me on frequent missions back to the UK. I have visited some fifteen different catering firms in the UK and Germany during that period.

2. I am applying for your vacancy because my husband and family are now returning home from Switzerland and I would like to remain in the modern business of food production and continue to use my up-to-date and international knowledge on behalf of a British company.

Yours faithfully

Elaine Chapman

Elaine Chapman (Mrs)

Enclosure

Example B

47

Application for a typist's job

>
> 17 East Road,
> Billford,
> Kent,
> MD7 OAP
>
> 4 May 1988

The Personnel Manager
Mercury Signs plc.

Dear Sir,

In answer to your advertisement in this morning's "Guardian" may I submit my application for the post of typist.

I am 19 years old and was educated at Knightly Comprehensive and the Tiphill Secretarial School. I have six 'O' levels including English and French. I can write Pitman's shorthand at one hundred words a minute, for which I have a certificate, and can use any make of word processor. I enclose two testimonials. This letter is a specimen of my typing.

Yours faithfully,

Viviane Harper

(Miss) Viviane Harper

   Obviously an application from a typist should be on good quality paper and immaculately typed.

A General Letter of Application

                                              32 Highfield Apartments,
                                                        Wimbledon,
                                                              London, S.W.19.

Box 2160,
c/o The Telegraph.
                                                             10 May 1988

Dear Sirs,

In answer to your advertisement in today's "Telegraph", I wish to apply for the position of Sales Manager.

I enclose my c.v. detailing my educational qualifications and work experience. In addition I would like to mention specifically that I have fifteen years experience working in the plastics industry including three years spent overseas.

I would be happy to call at your office at any time convenient to you.

Yours faithfully,

Letter resigning from a post

It is wise when resigning from any post to write positively about it and not to dwell upon any disagreements which may have led to the resignation. Past employers will become your future referees, and you do not wish to alienate them. It is likely that a polite letter of resignation will set the scene for better prospects in a new job.

> 2 Kenwood Square
> Pontland,
> Essex. EY2 AC3
>
> Paul Jones,
> Jones Antiques.
>
> Dear Mr. Jones,
>
> It is with some regret that I tender my resignation to take effect from 1st August next. I have accepted a post with E.J. Messon Ltd. and I shall be starting there in September.
>
> I would like to thank you for the support you have given me over the last four years. You have always been very fair and just. My new post gives me more scope and responsibility and I know that the valuable experience gained working with you has enabled me to achieve it.
>
> Yours Sincerely.

Testimonials and References

First let us be clear what these two terms mean.

1. Testimonials

These are written by previous employers and handed open to the ex-employee to carry about with him or her. They are useful to people contemplating a long period out of employment.

A typical testimonial reads like this:

```
To whom it may concern

Mrs Campion was employed by me as a housekeeper for ten years.  She is
clean, honest, hardworking and came to be regarded as one of the family.
We all wish her well in the future and know that whatever job she is
given she will do well and soon make herself invaluable.

                                 Sincerely,



                                 M. R. Horden
```

Sometimes a testimonial will suggest that the reader writes or telephones for a 'Reference' this may be well worth following up. Experience shows that often, 'honest' meant 'dull', 'hardworking' meant 'persistent' and 'one of the family' meant 'a pain in the neck'.

Sometimes testimonials are blunt and a well-known Royal Naval story goes that a Captain once wrote of a Junior Officer:

```
"To whom it may concern

Lieutenant X has for the last two years conducted himself entirely to his
own satisfaction, and has used my ship as a means of personal transport
from place to place."
```

2. References

References are confidential, and are written by 'referees' given to the prospective employer by the applicant. There are three dangers to applicants in selecting referees, which are seldom considered.

These are:

1. That the referees given are so obviously friends or relations of the applicant that their opinion is not objective enough to be valuable.

2. A referee (quite unknown to the applicant) does not like or support the candidate at all, and has been writing dreadful references about him or her for years. (N.B. If you persist in not getting short listed, change your referees).

3. A referee may write a good reference and even show it to the applicant but in a telephone conversation to the employer may hint that he or she is an unsuitable candidate.

Therefore, never ever take your chosen referees for granted, always try to see a copy of what has been written. It is usual for a prospective employer to request one professional and two business references.

Writing References

When asked to write references you should decide whether you really support the applicant. If so, then make it a point of honour to write so well that the applicant gets the job. Vague phrases like 'always been satisfactory', 'done a good job', 'renowned for punctuality', 'we shall miss him/her', 'very reliable worker' are all designed to send the recipient to sleep. Also most of these clichés quite clearly reveal the inadequacies of the candidate rather than the strong points.

A good reference is bold and arresting and starts straight away. For example:

PERCY BYSHE-FELTHAM

As a clerical assistant Mr. Byshe-Feltham is outstanding. One month after arriving in our office he had mastered a very complex filing system and then improved and updated it. This saved the Company several thousand pounds. His energy and enthusiasm are boundless and infectious. The whole atmosphere of an office improves when he comes in. This year he has been entirely responsible for programming our new and sophisticated computer system which has worked perfectly.

This Company will be much the poorer for his loss but his talents deserve wider scope in a much larger firm.

You would be well advised to appoint him as his kind of ability is rare, and he is undoubtedly headed for the top in business.

Please give me a phone call personally if you would like to discuss Mr. Byshe-Feltham's application further.

                              Yours etc.

Letters to the Press

Letters to newspapers and magazines are part of the entertainment business and should always be formulated with that rule in mind. Whether the subject is religious, political, academic or just finding the first cowslip in Tooting, a fairly light-hearted touch is best. Always remember that however strongly you feel about your chosen subject, ninety per cent of the readers will either be indifferent to it, or take the exact opposite viewpoint.

If your object in writing is to convince or convert, you need to read and re-read your own letter from the point of view of a severe critic. For example here are two letters on the same subject. Regardless of your own viewpoint decide which one would be the most effective.

1

> THE EDITOR
>
> Dear Sir
> Once again I see that this government has decided to force the torture of the eleven plus onto the nation's children. Bringing back the grammar schools may suit those rich families who can afford to pay for uniforms and private coaching. When I was a lad I was told I was a failure because I did not pass the exam. I left school at 14 feeling like a second class citizen and I do not want to see my grandchildren go through the same suffering through no fault of their own. Only snobs support this system and I say it is not fair on the ordinary working man.
>
> Yours faithfully

2

> THE EDITOR
>
> Dear Sir,
> I see that the hoary old chestnut that children of eleven years old can be graded into just two kinds is about to be resurrected, those with academic 'gifts' and those with a more 'practical' bent. How convenient it would be for us if this were really true. But the last thirty years has persisted in proving that many grammar school children fail both their 'O' and 'A' levels, and many secondary modern school children end up in Universities. Would it not be better as most of us experience in our families to encourage all our youngsters for as long as possible and let them sort themselves out in due course without being labelled 'swots' or 'failures' too soon in life?
>
> Yours faithfully,

It is most effective if you select with care which newspaper or magazine to write to. Every journal has a particular accent or interest. Obviously if you have a point to make about car repairs or looking after your dog, your letter would be more likely to be published in a motor magazine or a pet's weekly. By the same token, letters of concern about the law would be more likely to be accepted in a law gazette or a daily paper with a legal section, than in a sports magazine or fashion weekly.

Try not to air *just* your feelings, but collect some genuine evidence or statistics to support your case. A good firsthand experience will usually be published, but not hearsay or "Let me tell you what happened to a friend of mine". If the friend's experience was crucial then let the friend write the letter!

Example

> The Editor
>
> Dear Sir,
>
> I live in a London suburb where almost all the homes have large gardens. According to the local authority, twenty per cent of our residents are dog owners. In the last six months I have counted local dog owners walking their pets and encouraging them to foul the pavement on 350 occasions. I have stopped many of them and asked them to use their own gardens. They look at me as if I were mad. Why is it that people have such a blind spot about dogs, yet they would never allow children to do this? It is surely time that strict legislation was brought in to inhibit this anti-social and unhealthy practice.
>
> Yours faithfully,
>
> Dog Lover

Writing to your Member of Parliament

The mode of address to an ordinary MP is as to any other member of the public with the addition of MP after the name.

e.g. Jane Ashville MP

Dear Mrs Ashville,
etc. etc., and end Yours sincerely,

If you know the private address of your MP you may write there. You should certainly make sure you know his or her correct name and party before writing! It will generally be more effective if you write to the House of Commons, Westminster, London SW1 as there will be secretarial help and research facilities available to assist the MP with your query. Any problems may be brought to the notice of your MP and almost all are glad to help if they can. However, do make sure that you have tried the local and common-sense remedies first. A letter to your MP is best as a last resort, rather than as a first step as he or she will inevitably refer you back to the 'proper channels' if you have not tried them. For example, a complaint about litter in the park will be solved quickest by a letter to the local authority first.

If your MP is a Government Minister then you would address him or her by the 'office' e.g.

To The Secretary of State for Employment

Dear Sir/Dear Madam and end Yours faithfully,

If the Minister is personally known to you you may write:

Dear Minister
Dear Chancellor
etc.
and end Yours sincerely,

Conclusion

We hope you have enjoyed reading "Better Letters" and found out what fun letter writing can be. An effective response to a complaint, a cheerful reply from a friend both make the time and trouble spent learning to write better letters worthwhile. Letter writing is a practical art with many everyday applications so now it's over to you to make your skills personally profitable, effective and businesslike.

Range of Nibs

OSMIROID produce the world's largest range of fountain-pen nibs for fine writing, calligraphy, drawing and music writing.

Regular Right Hand

- Rola Extra fine
- Rola broad soft
- italic medium
- Rola fine soft
- italic extra fine
- italic broad
- Rola medium soft
- italic fine

Specialist Right Hand

- Rola medium hard
- SH6
- B5
- Long life tipped nib
- B6
- Copperplate
- B2
- B8
- SH4
- B3
- SH5
- B4
- B10

Regular Left Hand

Rola medium soft

italic medium

italic broad oblique

italic fine oblique

italic medium oblique

Specialist Left Hand

B2 oblique

B3 oblique

B4 oblique

INDIA INK

Sketch

Rola medium soft.

B2

Sketch BOLD

Rola broad soft.

B4

Music

italic medium

B6

    Many of the nibs illustrated are obtainable in a range of pen sets manufactured by Osmiroid for calligraphy, italic writing, drawing and sketching.

Arabic Available in Sets

عريض ٢
Broad 2

رفيعة جدًا ولينة
Very Fine Flexible

عريض ٣
Broad 3

رفيعة اكسترا
Extra Fine

عريض ٤
Broad 4

رفيعة
Fine

عريض ٥
Broad 5

متوسطة
Medium

عريض ٦
Broad 6

عريضة
Broad

Also available in the range of Osmiroid publications are:
The Osmiroid Book of Calligraphy
Making Calligraphy Work for You
Colour Calligraphy
The Art of Sketching
Pen and Ink Drawing
Chinese Brush Painting
The Art of Poster Making
The Art of Stencilling

the art of POSTER MAKING
by John Smith
EAST ANGLIAN ARTS SOC
EXHIBITION
Osmiroid Creat
the art of STENCILLING
by Helen Barnett
Creative Leisure Series
the art of SKETCHING
by Malcolm Macdonald
Osmiroid Creative Leisure Series

Designed by Nigel Long Design, Winchester.　　　　　　　　　　　　　　　　　　　　　　　　　　　　　　　　　　　　Printed in Spain